★ ★

The JIMMY CARTER Story

★ ★

(Next page) President Carter, daughter Amy and grandson Jason
in Amy's treehouse in a tree on the South Lawn of the
White House.

★★

The
JIMMY CARTER
Story

★★

by Margaret Poynter

Illustrated with Photographs

JULIAN MESSNER NEW YORK

Manufactured in the United States of America

Design by Alex D'Amato

PHOTO CREDITS
The White House: pp. 2, 11, 13, 22, 30, 50, 55, 75, 77, 79, 82, 83, 84-85, 86,
88-89, 90-91
Wide World Photos: pp. 12, 26, 37, 53, 60, 61, 64, 68, 71, 72, 73, 76, 81

Library of Congress Cataloging in Publication Data

Poynter, Margaret.
    The Jimmy Carter Story.

    Includes index.
    1. Carter, Jimmy, 1924-   —Juvenile literature.
2. Presidents—United States—Biography—Juvenile
literature. I. Title.
E873.P68   973.926'092'4   [B]   78-15757
ISBN 0-671-32945-6

★ ★

To my husband
You gave me the courage to enter
the magical world of writing.

★ ★ ★ ★ ★ ★ ★ ★ ★ ★ ★ ★ ★ ★ ★ ★ ★ ★ ★ ★

Contents

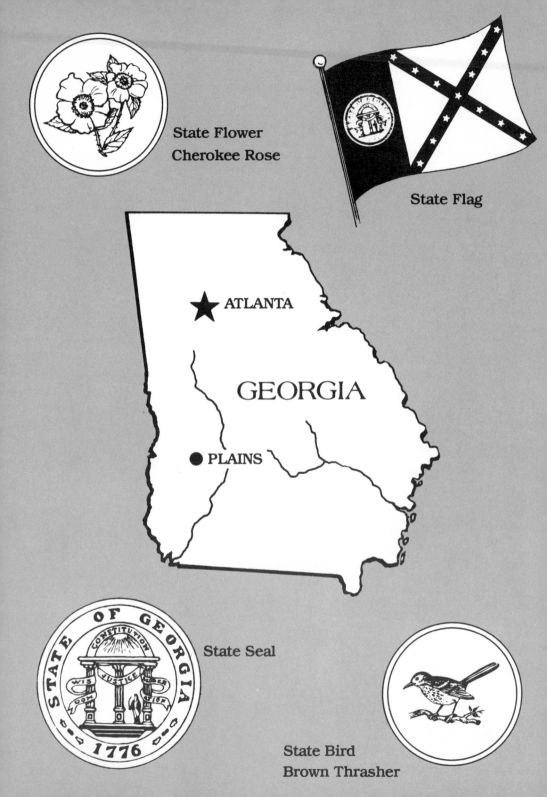

State Flower
Cherokee Rose

State Flag

ATLANTA

GEORGIA

● PLAINS

State Seal

State Bird
Brown Thrasher

"That's Just the Way Things Were"

Ten-year-old Jimmy Carter trudged up and down the rows of cotton, carrying a bucket and a small rag mop. The hot Georgia sun beat upon his bare back as buzzing swarms of flies bit his shoulders. Again and again, he dipped the mop into the bucket and daubed the mixture of molasses, arsenic, and water onto each bud of cotton.

The job was tiring, but the boll weevils had to be killed to save the crop. "Mopping" was the accepted way to get rid of the insects. By the end of the day, Jimmy was soaked with the sticky mess. When he took off his jeans, he stood them in the corner of his bedroom. The legs were too stiff to bend.

The Carter farm was just outside the small town of Archery, which is three miles west of Plains, Georgia. Jimmy's great-great grandfather had moved to Georgia in the late

1700s. Three generations later, the widowed mother of James Earl Carter settled in Plains with her five children. James Earl became a farmer, and later met and married Lillian Gordy, a local girl. Through his father-in-law, who was a politician, he became involved in community affairs.

Jimmy—James Earl Carter, Jr.—was born on October 1, 1924. Within seven years his two sisters, Gloria and Ruth, were born. Since his brother Billy didn't arrive until 1937, Jimmy became his father's chief "outdoor boy." He fed livestock, chopped wood, and pumped and hauled water. He learned how to repair tools in the family's blacksmith shop, and waited on customers in the Carter general store, which was next to their house.

These tasks had to be done every day. In addition, there were special jobs which came with each season. In the spring and summer, the farm bell rang at 4 A.M. Jimmy joined his father at the barn, and they rode out to the fields in a mule-drawn wagon. When Jimmy was small, it was his job to "tote" water and run errands for the field hands, or hired farm workers.

As he grew older, he helped to harrow, rake, pile up weeds, and plow. When the land was ready, he prepared and fertilized seed beds for the planting of corn, cotton, and peanuts. As the cotton buds appeared, Jimmy had to do the hateful mopping.

Most of Jimmy's friends were the sons of the black field hands. He spent all day working with them. As they bent over their rakes and shovels, they sang and talked. When Jimmy's work was done, much of his spare time was

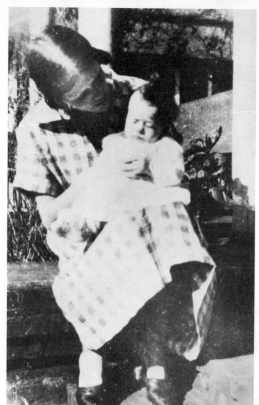

Six-months-old Jimmy
in his mother's lap.

"Hot" did all kinds of
outdoor chores.

Mr. Carter stands in the doorway of his store which was next to the house. In front of him are six-year-old Gloria, three-year-old Ruth, and eight-year-old Jimmy.

spent with A.D. Davis. Next to his father, Jimmy's best friend was A.D. They fished for catfish and eel, and built dams on the small streams in the woods. They rolled steel barrel hoops, slid down straw hills on old plow blades, and flew homemade kites.

They dug honey out of bee trees and picked wild plums, blackberries, and persimmons. They slept in a tree house. Late at night, they shivered as they remembered the blood-curdling tales they had heard from the old Indian who lived down the road.

From early April until the end of October, neither Jimmy nor A.D. wore a shirt or shoes except for going to church or to school.

During the harvest season, watermelons had to be cut and hauled to the train. Corn and cotton was picked by hand. Peanuts were pulled from the ground and stacked on poles to dry. Jimmy took some of the peanuts and washed the dirt from the hulls. After letting them soak in water all night, he boiled them in salt water and packed them in small paper bags.

On Saturday, he walked along the railroad tracks into the small, dusty town of Plains. There he sold his boiled peanuts for a nickel a bag. There were ten regular customers among the overalled checker players who sat around the service station, the garage and the livery stable. He had to sell the rest to strangers. It was hard for Jimmy to talk to someone he didn't know, because he was timid. One day he told his mother that he knew who the good people in Plains were.

Jimmy, with his colt Lady and dog Sam, in the back yard of the Carter home.

"Who?" she asked.

"They are the ones who buy my peanuts," Jimmy replied.

Jimmy and A.D. often walked into Plains on weekends and holidays. They could always join a group of boys in top spinning and marble playing. Sometimes there was a traveling medicine show in town. They never bought the bottles of medicine, but they liked to watch the free show. Sometimes there were log cutting contests put on by ax salesmen, and once a year a small circus came to town.

Winter was the time to slaughter the hogs and "cure" the meat. Sugarcane was cut and crushed, and the juice boiled down into syrup. Pine and hickory wood was chopped into logs for firewood. When school was in session, Jimmy had to hurry to get both his homework and his chores done.

Black and white children went to different schools, so Jimmy and A.D. could not spend all day together. Both of them accepted this separation the way they accepted the hard work they had to do. Everyone they knew worked in the fields, or helped out in the family business. No one had much money, and brothers and sisters wore each other's "hand-me-downs." Mr. Carter once ordered some women's boots to sell in his store. When no one bought them, Jimmy had to wear them to school.

Jimmy didn't know which time was worse—when he had to wear those shoes, or the time the mule shears slipped while his father was giving him a hair cut. A big gap was cut out of the hair on the top of his head. His father had to clip his head almost bald to make the hair even. Jimmy was so embarrassed, he wore a cap to hide his head. The following week he had to go to another city and visit his grandmother. Later his mother asked her what she thought of Jimmy.

"He's a fine boy," his grandmother said. "But he acts peculiar. He's the only child I've ever seen who ate and slept while wearing a cap."

Mrs. Carter worked twelve to twenty hours a day as a nurse. Both her patients and her friends called her Miss Lillian. With the help of Ruth and Gloria and a housekeeper, she took care of the six-room wooden clapboard house. As with most farm homes, there was no running water or electricity. The cooking was done on a wood stove, the heat provided by fireplaces, and the light by kerosene lamps. The Carters knew that they were lucky to have a good home and plenty to eat. The United States was in the middle of a severe depression. Many people had no jobs and were hungry.

In spite of their long hours of work, the Carters had time for fun. They had many friends and liked to give parties and have company for dinner. Jimmy was used to going to sleep with the sound of laughter filling the house.

Mr. Carter was honest and fair, and demanded that his children be the same way. When they weren't, they were punished. One Sunday morning, Jimmy got a penny from his father to put in the church collection plate. Instead of putting it in, Jimmy took one out. His father saw the two coins when they got home, and he reached for a long peach tree switch. Jimmy did not forget that whipping for a long time.

Mr. Carter called Jimmy "Hotshot," or "Hot" for short. He didn't like to give orders to his children. Instead, he gave suggestions, such as "Hot, would you like to turn the sweet potato vines this morning?"

Perhaps Jimmy did *not* want to turn the potato vines, but he usually replied, "Yes, sir, Daddy, I would." If he didn't get his work done, he was punished. One time he had to stay home from a family picnic to prune the watermelon patch.

Jimmy was often rewarded for doing a good job by being allowed to go to political rallies with his father. Jimmy liked these meetings. There were crowds of people, a lot of speech making, and plenty of free food.

Miss Lillian taught her children how important school and learning were. She often had a book open by her breakfast plate, and spent many evenings reading out loud to Mr. Carter, whose eyesight was poor. She would even forgive Jimmy and his sisters for not getting their work done, if they had been busy reading instead.

Miss Lillian also taught them something which was not popular in the South of the 1930s—to treat all people alike, regardless of the color of their skin. She shocked her friends by having blacks sit in her front room and serving them tea and cookies.

"Imagine that Miss Lillian," the people of Plains must have said. "Doesn't she know that Negroes are supposed to go around to her back door? And they should stand in the yard and talk to a white person—not go marching right into the house. Mr. Earl shouldn't put up with such goings on!"

If Jimmy heard the gossip, he didn't pay much attention to it. One time, however, he thought perhaps his mother was wrong. She had gone to a Buck Jones movie with him and A.D. Buck Jones was a popular cowboy star, and Jimmy's favorite actor. When they entered the theater, Miss Lillian pushed A.D. right past the usher and made him sit downstairs with the white people. Jimmy noticed that when his mother wasn't looking, A.D. slipped upstairs to sit in the "colored folks' section."

Jimmy knew how his friend felt. After all, everyone said the Negroes and whites weren't supposed to sit side by side in movie houses. Jimmy didn't know why. He figured that's just the way things were.

2

Dreaming of a
Different Sort of Life

In spite of his busy and happy life on the farm, Jimmy often dreamed of quite a different sort of life. He had an uncle, Tom Gordy, who was in the United States Navy. As his uncle visited foreign cities, he sent Jimmy packages and letters. Even before Jimmy entered the first grade, he had decided to become a sailor so he could see the world for himself.

Mr. Carter wanted all of his children to finish high school, and go on to college if possible. He himself had been forced to drop out of school in the tenth grade. Since money was always scarce in the Carter household, he told Jimmy about the fine free education which could be obtained at the military academies. Jimmy had read about the Naval Academy which is located at Annapolis, Maryland. Not mentioning that he was still in grammar school, he sent away for the Academy's catalog and entrance requirements.

When the catalog arrived, he read it so often that he soon had it memorized. Annapolis was the way to get the two things he wanted most—a good education and travel with the Navy. His main goal from then on was to become a midshipman at the Academy.

But once he made his decision, he wondered if the Academy would take him. Maybe he wasn't strong enough, or smart enough. Every day he laid a soda pop bottle on the floor and rolled his feet over it to strengthen his arches. He stuffed himself with fruit, vegetables, and meat because he was underweight.

When he chewed an apple, he realized that his teeth did not fit together properly. To help make up for that weakness, he brushed them often to keep them clean and healthy.

Jimmy had always liked to compete and win. When he went fishing, he was disappointed when he didn't make the biggest catch. He worked hard to become the fastest cotton picker in his father's fields. The fact that the field hands were unbeatable didn't stop him from trying. He hoped this trait would help him in the competition to get into the Academy.

Tarzan, the Hardy Boys, and stories of old West shoot-outs had always been among Jimmy's favorite reading. Now he started checking out books on science and history from the library. The more he read, the more he wanted to read. When anyone asked him what he wanted for Christmas or a birthday present, he answered, "Books!"

"Mama, I don't *ever* want to stop learning," he said one day.

His favorite teacher, Miss Julia Coleman, awarded

9 4/10/2

gold and silver stars, and bronze medals for book reports. She once asked Jimmy to read *War and Peace* and give a report on it.

He could hardly wait to start, because he thought that it would be about cowboys and Indians. He was disappointed when he found that instead it was about kings and emperors. But he was glad that he didn't put it back on the library shelf. He had learned an important lesson as he read the long book. It is ordinary people—farmers, shopkeepers, barbers, and soldiers—who determine what is going to happen in their country. Dictators and tyrants may enslave their subjects, but eventually the people can take matters into their own hands.

Jimmy thought that school was an exciting place. The students put on plays, entered essay contests, memorized and recited poems, had spelling bees, and took music lessons. Miss Julia believed that even farmers and clerks should know about music and art.

One of Jimmy's sixth grade assignments was to make a list of "healthy mental attitudes." Among the items he wrote down was "the habit of expecting to accomplish what you attempt." He knew that just wanting to go to Annapolis would not get him there. He had to work hard, too. His report cards showed a string of A's in everything from citizenship to carpentry and shorthand.

One of his proudest days was when he was sworn in as Schoolboy Patrolman. He wore a white canvas belt and sported a tin badge, as he made sure that his classmates obeyed the school safety rules. Included in his duties was running to the nearest house for help when the rickety "crackerbox" school bus slid off a muddy road into a ditch.

As he grew older, one of his jobs at home was to take care of his sisters when his mother and father went into town. "Jimmy, you're the boss now," Miss Lillian would say.

Baby-sitting was not one of Jimmy's favorite jobs. He spent much of the time quarreling with his sisters and teasing them. Once he gave Ruth a hot pepper.

"Taste it," he said. "It's real sweet."

Ruth took a big bite. Gasping and choking, she screamed that she was on fire. Jimmy doubled over with laughter. When his father came home and heard about Jimmy's joke, he went to the peach tree to cut a switch.

Jimmy was whipped again when he shot Gloria in the rear end with a BB gun. The fact that she had thrown a wrench at Jimmy didn't make any difference to Mr. Carter.

Jimmy had many fights with his sisters, but he would not allow anyone else to hurt them. Once an older boy purposely caused Gloria to fall and break her arm. Jimmy fought with the boy and won. The boy promised to stay away from Gloria forever.

In 1937, when Jimmy was thirteen, Billy was born. Jimmy must have been glad to have another boy in the family.

When Jimmy entered high school, he started taking girls out to parties and church dances. To earn money for these dates, he sold newspapers and scrap metal. He and his cousin Hugh put up a stand in Plains. They sold five-cent hamburgers and three scoops of ice cream for a nickel.

A few years earlier, Jimmy had bought five bales of

When he was fifteen, Jimmy attended a Future Farmers of America camp.

cotton with his peanut money. He paid five cents a pound for it, and was now able to sell it for eighteen cents a pound. Instead of spending the money, he bought some property with it.

Sometimes he and his friends rode the three-car train to Americus, a town thirteen miles east of Archery. When A.D. went along, he had to sit in a separate car. Segregation was still the rule in the South, and Jimmy had not once heard anyone question the system.

However, there were a few things which started bothering him. A.D. had started acting as if he were a servant and Jimmy were the boss. He ran ahead and opened doors and gates and let Jimmy enter first. A.D.'s mother started treating Jimmy as if he were "company," instead of one of the family. She even called him "*Mr.* Jimmy."

The changes made Jimmy uneasy. "Are you going to start calling me 'Mister'?" he asked A.D. one day.

A.D. grinned. "To tell you the truth, I don't *ever* know whether I'm gonna say 'mister' to y'all."

"I don't blame you," Jimmy replied. "I wouldn't either if I were you."

As he grew older, Jimmy found his life changing. One thing, however, remained the same—his desire to attend Annapolis. As high school graduation drew near, it looked as if all his hard work had paid off. He was at the top of his class, and was certain to become valedictorian.

Just a few days before graduation, a group of boys asked Jimmy to play hooky and go to a movie with them. He figured that missing one day of school wouldn't make any difference, and that no one would find out about it anyway. He went to the movie.

He was terribly wrong. Everyone found out about it. His father thrashed him. Even worse, Miss Julia dropped him to second place in the class. A girl became the valedictorian.

Two Dreams Come True

In 1942, Stephen Pace, a United States Congressman from Georgia, recommended Jimmy for an appointment to Annapolis. Congressman Pace knew of the Carter family because of Mr. Carter's support of certain farm legislation. All United States Congressmen are allowed to recommend ten young people for appointments to the military academies.

Jimmy was not to enter Annapolis until the following year. While he was waiting, he went to a college in Atlanta, which is the capital of Georgia. He took engineering and other courses which he thought would help him at the Academy. He also joined the Reserve Officers Training Corps.

As the year came to a close, Jimmy was worried because he was too thin. He quit a part-time job so he could get more rest. He studied in bed to save energy. He tried to "plump" himself by eating dozens of bananas. He still weighed only one hundred and twenty pounds when he entered Annapolis.

He had thought he was fully prepared for the Academy life. But he soon discovered there were two things he wasn't ready for. One of them was the feeling of homesickness. The other was the practice of "hazing," which means being forced to perform silly and unnecessary jobs. If the jobs are not done well, there may be painful punishments. In some clubs or schools, the older members haze the newer members. At Annapolis, the upperclassmen hazed the newcomers, or the "plebes."

Jimmy almost forgot what it was like to have a peaceful meal. If someone thought he had bad table manners, Jimmy was forced to eat under the table. If he had an expression on his face that an upperclassman didn't like, his food was taken away.

He was stopped in the hall and asked questions which had no real answers. He was ordered to write reports on foolish subjects. If he failed to follow the orders, he had to run the obstacle course at night.

Jimmy tried hard to please the hazers, but there was one order that he could not obey. He was told to sing "Marching Through Georgia," a song which tells of the South's defeat in the Civil War. Most Southerners hated that song.

Every day the upperclassmen asked Jimmy to sing the song. When he refused, he was called ugly names. He was forced to bend over and be paddled with a large serving spoon. He was also ordered to "shove-in." That meant he had to eat his meal in a regular sitting position, but not touching the chair.

Jimmy became angry at such treatment, but he did not show it. The only signs that he was angry were the clenching of his jaws, and the throbbing of the vein in his neck.

The upperclassmen never did hear him sing "Marching Through Georgia."

There were also regular punishments which the instructors handed out. Anyone who broke even the smallest of the many Academy rules had to do extra marching, or row a heavy boat until his arms ached.

Between the hazing and the official penalties, it was impossible for even the best behaved midshipman to stay out of trouble. It was hard to understand such a harsh system at the time. Later, however, Jimmy saw that there was a reason

Jimmy, on the left, while a midshipman at Annapolis.

for it. A military officer has to learn to take orders before he can become a good leader himself. He has to be able to stand up under hardships without losing his temper.

The United States was in the midst of World War II while Jimmy was at Annapolis. What he and his classmates learned might save their lives and the lives of the men they commanded when they went into battle.

An officer has to learn everything about the ship upon which he serves. The midshipmen spent days and nights studying about gunnery and weapons. They studied and practiced seamanship, navigation, astronomy, engineering, and naval tactics. They had to stand guard duty, which is boring and lonely. They also had to learn to recognize, in a fraction of a second, the outlines of hundreds of American and foreign ships and aircraft.

Jimmy still found time to read about such things as philosophy and theology. He listened to recordings of classical music which he bought with his small allowance. He also wrote many letters to his family.

Gloria's letters to Jimmy caused him to be teased by the other midshipmen. He begged her to be a little more respectful.

"Dear Gloria," he wrote. "Please do *not* call me "Hot," and please do not write to me on lined notebook paper with pencil."

Annapolis men had to learn many different things. Jimmy had to take ballroom dancing lessons and attend formal dinners. He did not like going to these dinners. After the meal, a midshipman's name was called. That unlucky person had to give a speech. Jimmy could never enjoy his meal. He didn't know which was worse—giving his own speech, or watching his friends suffer through theirs.

The Academy wasn't all work. Jimmy played on the under-140-pound football team, ran in cross-country races and track meets, and competed in boat races. He especially liked learning to pilot a seaplane.

Every summer the students went on long cruises, usually on old battleships. They sailed to the Caribbean Sea and visited Jamaica, Trinidad, Puerto Rico, and the Virgin Islands. The voyages were not pleasure trips, since there was a constant danger of attack from German submarines. Frequent enemy alerts sent Jimmy racing to man the anti-aircraft guns.

Much of the time was spent doing tiring, monotonous tasks. "Holystoning" was one of the worst jobs. It involved rubbing a white brick back and forth over the whole deck until the wood shone. Jimmy's special job was cleaning the rest room in the rear of the ship. It was a dirty, smelly task, and he hated it.

There was very little fresh water on board, so sea water had to be used for bathing and laundry. The minute "reveille" or the wake-up call, was sounded, men started washing down the top deck with great streams of salt water from hoses. Jimmy and his classmates who were sleeping on the top deck had to scramble out of the way. Otherwise they were drenched with the icy water. Jimmy thought he would give anything for a full night's sleep in a warm bed.

In the summer of 1945, just before his last year at

Annapolis, Jimmy took a short trip home. One day, he and a friend drove down the main street of Plains in a rumble-seated Ford. Jimmy spotted Ruth and another girl in the church yard. When he stopped to talk with them, Jimmy recognized Ruth's friend as Rosalynn Smith. She had visited the farm many times, but he had never paid any attention to her because she was three years younger than he was.

His friend suggested that the four of them go out together that night. Since Jimmy didn't have anything else to do, he agreed. His mother was still awake when he returned home after the date. He went to the refrigerator to get some milk.

"I took Rosalynn Smith out to the movies," he said after a moment.

"Do you like her?" his mother asked.

Jimmy nodded. "She's the girl I want to marry."

During the summer of 1945, there was a lot of talk about the expected United States invasion of Japan. In August, the crew heard over the ship's loudspeaker that President Truman had something very important to tell the nation. Hundreds of officers and enlisted men gathered on the steel decks to listen. Most of them were expecting a report on the all-out land and sea attack on Japan's mainland.

What the President actually said surprised everyone. A stunned silence greeted the news of the atomic bombings of the Japanese cities of Hiroshima and Nagasaki, and of the

Rosalynn Smith was 18 and Jimmy Carter, 21, when they were married in Rosalynn's church, the Methodist church in Plains, Georgia, on July 7, 1946. Rosalynn later adopted her husband's Baptist faith.

unbelievable destruction and death which resulted. Jimmy had never even heard of the atom bomb, which dealt the deadly blows.

Japan surrendered almost immediately. On August 14, Jimmy and his crewmates joined in a noisy celebration. The screams of the happy crowds in Times Square in New York City blared over the loudspeaker. "It's over! The war is over!" The words were shouted again and again.

When Jimmy went home on Christmas leave, he had decided to ask Rosalynn to marry him. Now that he knew he wouldn't have to go into battle, he thought they could have a happy life together.

He found that actually asking her was much harder than just thinking about it. Although he saw her every night, he didn't find the courage to blurt out the words until his leave was almost over. He was very disappointed when her answer was no.

"I'm still in college," she said. "And I don't know yet what I want to do with my life."

Jimmy returned to Annapolis and tried to forget his disappointment. Then he decided that he would not accept her refusal. The following February he asked her again. This time she said yes. The wedding date was set for July, the month after his graduation from Annapolis.

"Did You

Do Your Best?"

When Jimmy graduated, he ranked fifty-ninth in a class of eight hundred and twenty. He was proud to be an ensign in the Navy, and looked forward eagerly to his life in the military service.

He was first stationed on the USS *Wyoming*, then on the USS *Mississippi*. Both of them were battleships which were based at Norfolk, Virginia. They were used to test new communication and gunnery devices. While Jimmy was in port, he unloaded tested equipment and installed new equipment. While he was at sea, he was the officer in charge of electronics and photography.

Jimmy found that the Navy was not quite as he had imagined it. The ships on which he sailed were old and badly in need of repair. The crews were only two-thirds their normal size, and most of the men were dissatisfied with the service. Since the war had ended, they were not receiving enough money or supplies to do their jobs well.

Their unhappiness affected Jimmy. He began to dislike the long hours of drudgery, and the lack of excitement. He resented not being able to see Rosalynn, even when he was in port. She lived in an apartment in Norfolk, but they saw each other only a few days a month.

One happy event occurred during this time. Their first son was born in 1947. His name was John William, but they called him Jack.

There were days when Jimmy felt discouraged enough to quit the Navy. After two years had passed, it was time to choose his next assignment. He and Rosalynn finally decided on the submarine service. Jimmy hoped it would give him the challenge he wanted.

He was accepted by the submarine school, and the Carters moved to New London, Connecticut. That was where the U.S. Navy Submarine Base was located. When Jimmy started to attend the classes, he knew he had found what he wanted in his Navy life. The instructors were strict, and the work kept him busy. He and his classmates had to pay attention to every detail of the lessons. When a ship is underwater, there is often no chance to correct a mistake. Every man must know his job perfectly, and be able to make instant decisions.

Jimmy finished third in a class of fifty two. He was assigned to the submarine USS *Pomfret*, which was based at Pearl Harbor, on the Hawaiian island of Oahu. He and Rosalynn and the baby went to Plains for a short vacation. Rosalynn and Jack stayed there when he went to join his ship.

Two days after Jimmy arrived at Pearl Harbor, the *Pomfret* sailed for the Far East. The trip was made in one of the worst storms in the history of the Pacific Ocean. Huge waves washed over the decks. The ship pitched and rolled. Jimmy was seasick for five days. He had to carry a bucket with him everywhere he went.

For a while, radio contact with Pearl Harbor was lost. People there believed that the *Pomfret* had sunk, as several other ships had.

In spite of the storm, the *Pomfret* had to come to the surface every night. While its batteries were being re-charged, it ran on its diesel engines, which needed air. One night Jimmy was standing watch on the bridge. He hung onto the handrail and fought to keep his footing on the slippery deck. Suddenly a great wave towered over him. It broke with a deafening roar.

His feet were lifted from under him, and the force of the water tore his hands from the rail. He tried to swim, but could not. He could only thrash his arms around. When the wave finally retreated, he was relieved to feel something solid beneath him. He was sitting on the barrel of the submarine's five inch gun!

As soon as it was safe to let go, he slid onto the deck and made his way back to the bridge. He had been very lucky. If the ship had been tilted a few inches in another direction, he would have dropped into the darkness of the sea.

Jimmy liked the *Pomfret*, and felt that it and its crew were the best in the Navy. Every man had to learn every single part of the ship. They all studied submarine operation, warfare, and patrol. There could be no carelessness, because they all depended upon each other. Because of the cramped living quarters, they also had to consider each other's feelings.

The *Pomfret* spent two months along the China Coast, sailing between the British colony of Hong Kong and the Chinese city of Tsingtao. It also went to the Yellow Sea to take part in military maneuvers with other American and British ships.

At that time, the Chinese Communists and the Chinese Nationalists were at war with each other. The Communists had war camps in the hills above the cities. Within the cities, the windows of shops were boarded up, and people were afraid to walk on the streets. Old men and young boys were kidnapped by the Nationalists and forced to fight for them.

When the *Pomfret* came into port for supplies, it was tied at the pier with its bow facing toward the sea. That way it could move out quickly in case of trouble.

Rosalynn and Jack moved to Honolulu in April of 1949, so they could be with Jimmy when he returned to Pearl Harbor. A second son, James Earl Carter III, was born at the base hospital in 1950. The nurses called him "a chip off the old block," and Chip became his nickname. Because Jimmy's ship spent so much time at sea, he was not able to see his family as much as he wanted to. He had to learn how to spend a few days in a way that would make up for weeks of separation.

The *Pomfret* sailed to San Diego, California, where Jimmy's mother and father visited him and his family for a short time. Jimmy's next move was back to New London. Rosalynn joined him, and their third son, Jeffrey, was born there in 1952.

Jimmy had been called to New London to help design and build a new kind of submarine, the USS *K-1*. It was to be small and very quiet. Its special job was to fight other submarines underwater. Jimmy had to develop diving and surfacing methods and to plan for necessary supplies. He also had to decide where the crew would eat and sleep, and how to care for equipment in very cramped spaces.

For many months, he was the only Navy officer working with a crew of civilians. Just before the *K-1* was finished, other officers began to work on it. Jimmy became friends with them before they all went to sea to test it out.

The first time the *K-1* submerged, everyone took off his shoes, so there would be as little noise as possible. No one talked, because they wanted to test out the long range listening devices, or "sonar." The men were amazed at what they could hear. There were sounds from small fish nearby, and large ships many miles away.

Jimmy had not been in the Navy long enough to be commander of his own ship. However, since he had helped to build the *K-1*, he felt as if it was his duty to take care of it. The *K-1*'s captain said Jimmy "combed the bugs out by aptitude, hard work, and plain iron will."

On one of the *K-1*'s ocean trips, one man went crazy with "claustrophobia," (klah-stroh-foh-bee-uh) which is the

Lt. Jimmy Carter peers at instruments on submarine USS K-1.

fear of being in a small space. He had to be tied into his bunk so he wouldn't hurt himself or anyone else. As soon as possible, the ship was brought to the surface, and the man was taken away in a helicopter.

Sometimes Jimmy played cards with the other crew members. He spent much more time reading in his bunk. Jimmy was known as a "loner." When the men were allowed to go onshore, Jimmy would "stand in the background, smile, and watch us, and then bail us out if there was any trouble," as one crewman said.

In 1952, when Jimmy was twenty-eight, he became interested in the Navy's plans for two atomic, or nuclear, submarines. They were to be called the *Nautilus* and the *Seawolf*. Admiral Hyman Rickover had been working on the ideas for these new ships for several years. He believed that atomic power could be used to run submarines. Many people opposed him, but Rickover was tougher and more stubborn than they were. He convinced the top officers in the Navy that they should provide money to build the ships.

Even before Jimmy met Rickover, he wanted to work for him. He liked people who didn't give up or become discouraged. He also wanted to work on an atomic submarine. He talked to Rosalynn, and she agreed that he should try to be transferred from the *K-1*. Finally he got an appointment to talk to Admiral Rickover.

Jimmy was shown into a large room. The grim-faced admiral told him to sit down. "Just tell me about the subjects that you know best, Lieutenant Carter," he said.

Jimmy talked about familiar subjects such as current events, seamanship, literature, and naval tactics.

Rickover asked him some questions about those subjects. First the questions were easy, then they were harder.

"How did you stand in your class at the Naval Academy," Rickover asked.

Jimmy thought the admiral would congratulate him when he heard about his good record.

There were no congratulations. "Did you do your best?" asked Rickover.

Jimmy thought of the times when he could have studied harder than he did. "No sir. I didn't *always* do my best."

The admiral turned his back toward Jimmy. "Why not?" he asked. He said nothing more.

The interview lasted for two hours. When Jimmy left the room, he was certain that Rickover would never choose him to work on an atomic submarine. He was wrong, however. He was selected to be the senior officer of the *Seawolf*. The Carters moved to Schenectady, in eastern New York. Here Jimmy and three other officers helped build the *Seawolf* "prototype," which was one of the models from which other nuclear submarines would be built.

During the day, Jimmy taught classes in math, physics, and the operation of nuclear engines. At night, he studied atomic science. Everyone who worked on the *Seawolf* had to learn as much as he could.

Admiral Rickover made everyone work very hard. Sometimes they worked eighty-four hours a week. He expected everyone to do his job perfectly. However, he himself worked longer and harder than anyone else.

A Death in the Family and a Decision

During the following year, Jimmy traveled to Idaho to talk to the men who were building the *Nautilus* prototype. He went to Washington D.C. to see the people at the Atomic Energy Commission. He went to Chalk River, Canada, where there had been an accident with a nuclear reactor. Nuclear energy, which is made in nuclear reactors, is harmful to the health of anyone who comes in close contact with it. At Chalk River, Jimmy and two other men were exposed to the deadly energy as they worked on the damaged reactor. But their exposure lasted too short a time for them to be injured.

In 1953, he received an emergency message. His father was dying of cancer. He left Rosalynn and their sons in Schenectady, and rushed to Plains.

There had been many changes in his family in the

eleven years he had been gone. Ruth and Gloria were married and had children. His parents had moved from the farm into a house in Plains. Billy was sixteen and anxious to leave home to look for excitement.

Miss Lillian had been trying to take care of her husband and manage his peanut warehouse, where the neighboring farmers bought and sold crops. She was glad that Jimmy had come home to help her.

Jimmy sat by his father's bed for a long time. As they talked, many visitors and friends came with food, flowers, and messages.

When Mr. Carter died, people came from long distances for his funeral. Flowers filled the house. "Mr. Earl will be greatly missed," everyone said.

Jimmy stayed to help his mother get her money and business problems straightened out. He found that the Carter family did not have a lot of money. Many people had done business at the warehouse and had not paid their debts to Mr. Carter. He had not even tried to collect them. He had also given away money to students who needed it to finish school.

Jimmy could see why everyone loved his father so much. Through his business and his generosity, he had helped the whole town. He had also been a good husband and father.

What about me? Jimmy wondered. My life is so different from what his was. The Navy gives me a good income. Rosalynn and my sons will never be poor. My work is exciting, and I am able to travel around the world.

But I do not see my family very much. We do not have

a real home. All I think about is my work. Everyone I know is in the Navy.

"I wonder if I have the sort of friends our father had," he said to Gloria. "If I died, nobody would care. Not *really* care."

By the time Jimmy returned to Schenectady, he had decided to leave the Navy. Rosalynn did not like the idea, and they had their first serious quarrel. Rosalynn liked the Navy life. She thought that someday Jimmy would be an admiral. And she didn't want to go back to Plains.

They argued far into the night, and Rosalynn finally gave up. It was two o'clock in the morning when Jimmy telephoned his mother.

"I'm coming home," he said.

The next step was to tell Admiral Rickover. Rickover was very angry. He thought that Jimmy was being foolish to give up his rank as lieutenant. But Jimmy did not change his mind.

Jimmy and his family returned to Plains in the winter of 1953. It was not a happy event. They had saved some money, but Jimmy did not have a job. Many people owed money to his father's business, but they could not pay it. Their crops had failed because there had not been enough rain.

To start earning money right away, Jimmy sold fertilizer. He spent long hot days shoveling it into large bags, then loading the bags onto his customers' trucks.

The times were hard for Miss Lillian also. Billy missed his father, and he was not willing to take orders from Jimmy.

When he graduated from high school, he joined the Marines, then married his high school sweetheart. Miss Lillian found that with her children no longer at home and Jimmy taking care of the business, she did not have enough to do.

"I can't just sit around," she said. To keep busy, she became a fraternity housemother at a university, then later opened up a small nursing home in a nearby town.

Jimmy decided to start growing a special kind of peanut. He sold the seeds from these peanut vines to other farmers, then bought the crops back from them. He found that he had to learn more about modern farming methods, and spent his evenings studying and taking classes. Rosalynn became his bookkeeper. During the harvest season, they both worked eighteen to twenty hours a day.

"Jimmy never sat on his bottom and waited for business," one of his friends said.

In the slower times of the year, Jimmy and Rosalynn were able to visit old friends and make new friends. The whole family attended Jimmy's old church, Plains Baptist, and he became a deacon of the church.

Both Jimmy and Rosalynn grew to like their new life. However, signs of trouble began to appear. In 1954, the members of the United States Supreme Court said that racial segregation must end. Black and white children should be allowed to go to the same schools. All white churches had to admit black members.

Many white Southerners were angry. They were afraid that their way of life would be greatly changed. There was an integrated farm near Plains. Someone set fire to it because it was owned by both black and white people. There were other violent acts during this time.

Jimmy believed that segregation should end. He told everyone what he believed, although that was a dangerous thing to do. Many people stopped coming to his warehouse. One afternoon a black woman brought a wagonload of peanuts to sell. There were a few white men ahead of her, but Jimmy waved her to the head of the line.

"You fellows don't mind if a lady goes through first, do you?" Jimmy asked.

Most of them did mind. One of them never came to the warehouse again.

The Plains White Citizens' Council was organized to fight school integration. The police chief tried to talk Jimmy into joining the council. When Jimmy refused, the chief became angry. "Every white man in the community has joined," he said. "That is, everyone except you."

Jimmy's friends said that they would pay his dues if he would join.

"I'll leave Plains before I'm forced to join any White Citizens' Council," Jimmy said.

Rosalynn found out that the son of one of the white members of the integrated farm had died. A white Baptist minister refused to speak at the funeral service, but Rosalynn talked him into conducting the service. She also helped the dead boy's family through the sad time.

People showed their disapproval of such actions by not coming to the warehouse. Jimmy and Rosalynn needed the money, but they would not change their minds. They thought that many white people probably felt the way they did, but were afraid to say so.

Except for two or three people, the customers soon returned. Within a few weeks, business was almost back to normal.

Once again, Jimmy and Rosalynn started going to parties and square dances. Jimmy went to stock car races, and on sunny weekends the whole family went to the beach. Jimmy joined the Sumter County School Board so he could work for better schools. He also joined the Lions' Club, which gives help to people when they are in need.

But something was wrong. Jimmy was bored. He missed having problems to solve. Even when he went to a party, he didn't have any fun.

He was only 37 years old. He began to wonder if he would be dissatisfied and restless for the rest of his life.

6

Headfirst into Politics

As Jimmy looked for a way to get over his restlessness, he thought about politics. His father and his grandfather, Jim Jack Gordy, used to talk about political decisions which affected them. Congress had passed laws which set up the Civilian Conservation Corps, which had given jobs to many farm boys. Laws had also been passed which gave farmers free mail delivery, and had brought electricity to the rural areas. All of these things made the life of a farmer easier.

Jimmy's father had served in the Georgia state legislature the year before his death. He had told Jimmy that it was one of the most worthwhile experiences of his life.

The 1963 Georgia Senate race was coming up, and Jimmy decided to enter it. A visiting minister tried to discourage him. He said that many people thought that all politicians were dishonest.

"Perhaps you should become a minister or work in some kind of social service," he said.

Jimmy knew that there were many honest politicians, and he could be one of them. A friend was with him when he went to sign up as a Democratic Party candidate.

"Should I write 'James Earl Carter, Jr.' or 'Jimmy Carter?' " Jimmy asked.

"For crying out loud," the friend replied, "it's *Jimmy*!"

Grinning, Jimmy signed the application. "Jimmy Carter."

Billy, who was now out of the Marines, offered to take care of the warehouse. His help enabled Jimmy and Rosalynn to enter upon a whirlwind campaign.

Both of them were shy around strangers, and did not like to travel to different towns to talk to people. They hated to give speeches. Many times they felt like going back home and forgetting about politics.

But that would mean that Jimmy would have to give up helping people. He wanted to build better schools, and see that segregation ended throughout the state. More and more people believed in the same things that he did, and offered to help him in his campaign. Jimmy did not want to disappoint them.

The day of the primary election arrived. In the primary, the voters choose the people who will run in the final, or general, election. Jimmy spent the day visiting the polling places of the towns in his district. He could hardly believe what he saw in Georgetown, a little town 50 miles west of Plains. All of the election laws were being broken. There were no voting booths where people could vote secretly. Instead, they were filling out paper ballots on the table as the local political boss watched them.

The boss kept pointing to a picture of Homer Moore, who was Jimmy's opponent. "This is a good man, and my friend," he said. After the voters put their ballots in a box, the boss pulled them out and looked at them.

Jimmy telephoned the editor of the local newspaper to report the dishonesty. No one paid any attention to him. When the ballots were counted that night, all of the 433 votes were for Homer Moore.

Jimmy found out that there were only 300 people who were allowed to vote in that town. So at least 133 of the votes must have been dishonest. He thought it would be easy to overturn the election, and get his name on the ballot for the general election.

He was wrong. Someone destroyed the ballots. Jimmy and his friends looked for more proof of the dishonesty, but they were constantly followed and threatened. People were afraid to talk to them. There was always someone standing nearby and listening.

A few people did say that their names had been signed as having voted, when they had not voted at all. Jimmy also found that many of the "voters" on the list had moved out of town or died long ago.

His enemies called him a "sore loser." The leaders of Georgetown said that he had no business telling them what to do. Appeals to state officials were ignored. Moore was declared to be the Democratic nominee for the general election.

Although Jimmy had very little time left, he continued his search for proof that Moore's election was illegal. Two lawyers, Warren Fortson and Charles Kirbo, worked day and night to help him. Moore and his friends worked just as hard to stop Jimmy. At almost the last minute, Jimmy convinced Georgia's Secretary of State that he should be the nominee. But the ballots had already been printed with Moore's name on them. What could Jimmy and his friends do? With only two days until the general election, they stamped Jimmy's name on all of the ballots from his district.

Jimmy won the general election and became the new state senator. Sick and exhausted, he spent the day after the election in bed.

Jimmy, Rosalynn, and their sons moved to Atlanta, and Jimmy was soon very busy at his new job. He had promised the voters that he would read every bill that he was to vote on. Since the Senate passed eight hundred to one thousand bills during every forty day session, Jimmy was glad that he had taken a speed reading course a few months earlier.

He found himself working five days a week instead of the four which most of the other senators worked. Jimmy was glad he worked the extra day, because he found many mistakes which the writers of the bills had made.

Jimmy Carter served two terms, or four years, in the State Senate. He opposed laws which gave special favors to politicians and their friends. He worked to improve the care of patients in Georgia's mental hospitals. He helped pass some laws which would prevent dishonest elections, and

Despite his busy schedule as a Georgia state senator, Jimmy found time to visit the family peanut warehouse in Plains.

others which would give children better schools. He worked for prison reform.

He constantly fought for the wise spending of the people's tax money. He knew that if elected officials were careful, they could give the people what they needed and still save money.

While he was a senator, Jimmy did many of the things he wanted to do. However, he lost some of his battles. He realized that many senators had never been poor, or out of work, or in a prison, or a mental hospital. Most of them had never even talked to such people, and they had no idea what sort of problems these people had. He felt that if the senators did know, they would pass the right sort of laws.

Jimmy was very busy in Atlanta, but he could not forget the problems of Plains. Civil rights leaders there were trying to force the white churches to admit blacks. The members of these churches did not like to be told what to do. Even the officers of Jimmy's own church had voted to keep the membership all-white.

When Jimmy heard about the vote, he rushed home to speak to a crowded church conference. He hoped he could get the members of the congregation to change their minds. Miss Lillian sat in the front row as he talked. She knew that Jimmy was angry.

"This is not my house," he said. "It is not your house. I believe that I can keep anyone out of my house that I want, and you can. But I for one will never stand in the doors of this church and keep anyone out."

When the vote was taken, there were only six people in favor of integration. Five of them were members of the Carter family. Many people had not voted at all, and Jimmy thought that they might agree with him, but were afraid to say so.

Before Jimmy left the Senate, he was chosen one of the five best state senators by the senators themselves. One day in 1965, he was talking to a friend. "You really ought to go on to better things," his friend said. "You ought to run for lieutenant governor."

Jimmy thought for a moment, then grinned. "Why *lieutenant* governor?"

"Jimmy Who?"

Jimmy did not really think he was ready for the high office of governor. Instead, he started to campaign to become a United States Senator. Billy and many of Jimmy's friends did not like his decision.

"You should enter the governor's race," they said. "If you do, we'll help you."

Some newspapers printed stories saying that Jimmy Carter was going to run for governor. People began to talk about the idea, and soon even Jimmy was thinking seriously about the governorship.

He had to make a difficult decision. It was 1966, and there were only three months left until the state primary election. He was hardly known outside of his own Sumter County. He didn't have much money. And he had no powerful friends. Two of his opponents in the race would be Ellis

Arnall and Lester Maddox. Both of them were well known, and had many rich friends.

Even a *famous* Democrat would have a hard time getting elected in the South at that time. Many white Southerners were angry at Democratic President Lyndon Johnson, because he was in favor of desegregation and civil rights for all people. These Southerners were almost certain to vote for the popular Republican, Howard Calloway.

The Carter family's views on segregation were well known. Miss Lillian had worked to get President Johnson elected. Unknown people had damaged her car, and sent

Jimmy plays football with two of his three sons.

ugly notes to her. Chip had worn a Johnson button to school, and had been beaten up by some older boys.

In spite of the problems, Jimmy decided to run for governor. When he announced his candidacy, many people wondered who he was. Newspapers published articles in which he was called "Jimmy Who?"

The whole Carter family helped in the campaign. Ruth and Gloria wrote letters, and talked to many people about their brother. Jack, Chip, Jeff, and Rosalynn traveled to different towns to put up posters and hand out brochures. So did Miss Lillian, although she was going to leave for India in just a few weeks. She had joined the Peace Corps, which is a group of men and women who are sent by the federal government to other countries to help people in need. Jimmy envied his mother for being able to do this kind of work.

Miss Lillian went from town to town. She walked up to people on the street and said, "I'm Lillian Carter, and I hope you'll vote for my son, Jimmy."

As the Carters talked to people, they asked them what they would like the government to do for them. They told everyone that Jimmy would be the servant of the people, not the master. He would try to give good schools and jobs and hospitals to poor people, as well as rich.

When election day came, Jimmy was prepared for the possibility that he might lose. However, when he heard that *both* Maddox and Arnall were ahead of him, he cried.

Jimmy went back to Plains and the peanut business. He kept asking himself, "What did I forget to do?" "How could I have turned the tide in my favor?" He blamed himself

Ruth, Senator Carter, Miss Lillian, Billy and Rosalynn.

for letting his family and friends down.

Losing the governor's race was not the only thing that was bothering Jimmy. He felt that there was something very important missing from his life. But he didn't know what it was.

He tried to find the answer when he went to church every week. During one of the services, the minister said, "If you were arrested for being a Christian, would there be enough evidence to convict you?"

Jimmy wondered if *he* would be convicted for being a Christian. He had gone to church all of his life, and had taught Sunday School since he was eighteen. He had served as deacon, and had taught the men's Bible class. But why was he so troubled? Why had his defeat left him so depressed? Why wasn't he happy even when he was with Rosalynn and the boys?

Jimmy knew that Rosalynn would not be able to help him find the answers. He had to find them by himself.

A month after his defeat, he started to campaign for the next election. It was almost four years away, but Jimmy had a lot of work to do. Even as he made his plans, he worried about the important thing that was missing in his life.

He remembered how calm and untroubled his sister Ruth had been during the hectic days of the campaign. She seemed to be happy, no matter what was happening. Jimmy asked her to come and see him.

Ruth thought she knew what was wrong with her brother. Although she had a husband and four children, she had also once felt troubled and dissatisfied. She found the answer to her problems through her religion.

She asked Jimmy many questions about the things that were important to him—his family, his business, and his political ambitions. She then asked him if he was willing to put Jesus Christ above all of those things.

"I would rather have the fullness of Christ in my life than be the President," Jimmy replied.

"You don't have to give up politics to be a Christian," Ruth said. "But you have to be the best politician you can possibly be."

Jimmy now knew that he had to do more than go to church once or twice a week. He had to help other people besides his friends and members of his own family. He had to be a Christian seven days a week.

He took time from his campaign and his business to make missionary trips to different places in Georgia, and to the northeastern part of the United States. He found he was no longer afraid to talk to strangers. When he shook their hands, he had a feeling of "instant togetherness."

"Jungle Jimmy," Governor of Georgia

One of the happiest days in Jimmy's life was October 19, 1967. On that day Amy Lynn was born. After twenty-one years of marriage, and three almost grown sons, Jimmy and Rosalynn had a daughter.

"Amy has made us young again," Jimmy wrote in a book which told of his life. "Her three brothers are so much older it is almost as though she had four fathers, and we have to stand in line to spoil her."

"I'm so happy," Miss Lillian wrote from India. "Oh, how I wish I could see her!"

Jimmy enthusiastically continued on his second campaign for governor. He worked at the warehouse until mid-afternoon. Later in the day, he studied so he could learn all about Georgia. He read books on its environment, its hospitals, its prison and court system, and its schools.

In the evenings, he traveled to nearby towns to discuss these subjects with various groups of people.

Some of his friends thought he was being too ambitious. They did not want him to be disappointed again. "Maybe you should try for lieutenant governor," they said. "Or how about commissioner of agriculture?"

But Jimmy had made up his mind to be governor. During the next three years, he gave 1800 speeches and shook 600,000 hands. One of the hands belonged to a department store dummy. When he realized what he had done, he grinned. "Give her a brochure," he said to a helper.

When Jimmy was campaigning far from Plains, he liked to spend the nights at the homes of local citizens. This gave him a chance to talk with them about the issues.

Jimmy's many friends were also trying to get him elected. They included Hamilton Jordan, who had just come back from doing volunteer work in Vietnam; Charles Kirbo, a lawyer; and Jody Powell, a college student. Jimmy was glad to have their help. His chief opponent in the primary was Carl Sanders, a former Georgia governor. Sanders had many powerful friends such as newspaper editors, judges, bankers, and lawyers, who did not like the changes in government that Jimmy wanted to make.

People such as farmers and factory workers were the ones most likely to vote for Jimmy. He also had the support of many young people who believed that blacks and whites should share the same schools, jobs, and opportunities. All of them wanted and needed the kind of government that Jimmy Carter talked about.

State Senator Jimmy Carter, with his campaign workers in Atlanta, going over the returns from the state primary.

Once a man came up to Jimmy after he had given a speech on the care of the mentally retarded.

"I'm going to vote for you," the man said. "Do you know why?"

"Why?" Jimmy asked.

"Because I have a retarded baby."

On another occasion Jimmy asked a young black woman what her name was.

"I ain't nobody," she replied.

Some of the people standing nearby laughed. Jimmy did not. "You are not a nobody," he said. "In fact, you are the reason I am running for office."

Jimmy and Rosalynn talked to people at football games

and rodeos, in beauty shops and supermarkets, in factories and in department stores. This time their efforts won Jimmy the primary election. He beat Sanders. He then went on to win the general election against the Republican candidate, Hal Suit.

At the age of forty-seven, Jimmy was the new governor of Georgia.

The inaugural ceremony was held in Atlanta on January 12, 1971. Three-year-old Amy stood beside her parents as it began. Right away, there was a surprise for the

Democratic nominee for governorship of Georgia, Jimmy Carter, and his wife, Rosalynn, as Carter claims victory in a runoff election. Jimmy beat former Governor Carl Sanders for the nomination, and Republican candidate Hal Suit in the general election on November 3, 1970.

audience. It had been the tradition to have a white band play "Dixie," a favorite song of white Southerners. This time a choir made up of black men and women sang "The Battle Hymn of the Republic," which is considered to be a "Yankee," or Northern song.

Jimmy's speech surprised many people, too. "We cannot afford to waste the talents and abilities given by God to one single person. . . . *I say to you quite frankly that the time for racial discrimination is over.*"

Jimmy believed that once the needed changes were made, hardly anyone would want to return to segregation and intolerence. Whites, as well as Blacks, had spent too much time worrying about the color of a person's skin. If they could forget about such things, they would have more time and energy for important projects.

While he was governor, Jimmy always arrived at his officer no later than 7:15 in the morning. He often stayed at his desk all day, eating a sandwich for lunch while he kept working. At night he went home with a briefcase full of papers to work on after dinner. The long hours didn't tire him. He was doing what he wanted to do.

A governor has to get the approval of the state legislature before he can put his ideas into operation. Jimmy never presented an idea until he was ready. He read everything he could find on the subject. He talked to experts and to citizens all over the state to get their opinions. He wanted to be prepared to answer any question that could be asked.

Jimmy wanted the members of the legislature to discuss his ideas with him. When he had made up his mind, however, he found it hard to change. If he was sure he was right, he argued with the people who opposed him. Many times tempers grew hot, and voices were raised. Jimmy became known as "Jungle Jimmy," because of his stubborn, fighting spirit.

"He's the sort of guy who comes upon a brick wall and goes into it full speed ahead," someone once said. "He doesn't want to hear the reasons why something can't be done."

One of the biggest battles between Jimmy and the legislators was his plan to reorganize the state government. He thought that there were too many state departments, many of them doing almost the same job. Even though his plan faced a lot of opposition, Jimmy would not give up. "He was standing there with the tide rushing over him," one man said.

In the end, Jimmy's plan won by a single vote.

Governor Carter made state officials spend the tax payer's money carefully. He, himself, thought of new ideas to save money. A herd of cattle was put to graze on the lawn of a large state hospital. The money that was saved by not having to mow the lawn was used for better patient care.

Under Jimmy's direction, there were reforms in the prison and justice systems, and improvements in the schools. Long before many Georgians were aware of water and air pollution, Jimmy was trying to protect Georgia's environment. He also worked to preserve its historical sites and its wildlife.

"It would be a bitter shame," he said, "if all this

Governor Jimmy Carter of Georgia and his wife, Rosalynn, chat with Governor Kenneth M. Curtis of Maine during the Democratic Governors' meeting in St. Louis.

natural beauty were not preserved for our children's children's children to view with joy one hundred years from now."

Jimmy made many trips around the state, and often visited local radio stations. The listeners were invited to call in and share their ideas with him. He also set aside one day each month when anyone could visit him in his office.

He and Rosalynn traveled to Brazil, Britain, and Israel. They invited citizens of those countries to come to Georgia and start businesses there. In this way, Jimmy thought, the people of Georgia could become acquainted with people from other countries.

Before Jimmy left office, he ordered three new portraits to be hung on the capital wall. One of them was of Martin Luther King, Jr., a famous black civil rights leader. The others were of Lucy Laney and Bishop Henry Turner. They were both Blacks who had played important parts in the history of Georgia.

Before those portraits were hung, all of the pictures on the wall had been of white Georgians. To Jimmy, the three new pictures were a symbol of how far the people of Georgia had advanced in a very few years. He knew there was still much work to do, but at least now Blacks and Whites could work together to get the job done.

★ ★ ★ ★ ★ ★ ★

9

★ ★ ★ ★ ★ ★ ★

"I'm Jimmy Carter, and I'm Running for President"

"President Jimmy Carter." It had sounded strange the first time Jimmy thought of it. By 1972, however, he had made up his mind. He wanted to be President of the United States.

Many people thought he should not try. He was a farmer, and farmers did not get elected to the highest office in the land. He was from the Deep South. No one from his section of the country had been president for over a hundred years. Also, Jimmy was almost unknown outside of his own state, and he was not familiar with national politics.

Jimmy did not change his mind. He knew that he could at least get the farmers' votes. He was used to overcoming obstacles and working hard. He thought that the voters would judge him by what he was instead of where he came from. He could study and learn about how the national government worked.

"But you're as stubborn as a South Georgia turtle," said Ben Fortsen, the Georgia secretary of state. "Doesn't a President have to be able to compromise?"

Jimmy said that he could change his mind, but only when he was proven wrong.

He continued having trouble getting people to take him seriously. Miss Lillian returned from India before his term as governor had ended. "Watcha gonna do when you're not governor?" she asked.

"I'm going to run for President," Jimmy replied.

She laughed. "President of *what*?"

"Mama, I'm going to run for President of the United States, and I'm going to win."

Rosalynn knew that Jimmy could do anything he set out to do. She was already busy helping him to plan his campaign. So were Hamilton Jordan and Jody Powell and many other friends.

"For our nation—for all of us . . . (the) question is, why not the best?"

It was December of 1974, and fifty-year-old Jimmy Carter was announcing his candidacy. Some of his opponents laughed. They called him the "upstart from Plains." "Jimmy Carter is running for *What*?" read one newspaper headline.

When he appeared on a national television show, no one knew who he was.

Many of his opponents were well known. One of them was Sargent Shriver, who was a relative of the slain President, John F. Kennedy.

Jimmy had a big job to do. He had to introduce himself to the whole country. But before he could do so, he had to become more familiar with the whole country. He started by working a jigsaw puzzle of the United States, so he would know exactly where every state was.

Within the next few months, he made speeches in over half of those states. He hardly even stopped to eat. Instead, he gulped hamburgers and milk shakes as he rushed from one place to another.

He never had enough money. Charles Kirbo told him that he was going to have to ask people to help him. To Jimmy that seemed like begging, but he and Rosalynn each made forty telephone calls every week to ask people for money.

"Hello, I'm Jimmy Carter, and I'm running for President. I need your help," he said again and again. He knocked on doors and shook hands, as he repeated the words all through the campaign. Chip, Jack, and their wives joined Rosalynn in her travels all over the country. Jeff worked at Jimmy's Atlanta campaign headquarters, while Miss Lillian took care of eight-year-old Amy.

Jimmy talked to anyone who would listen to him. On one cold day, in New Hampshire, the only audience he could find were some fifth graders. They were more interested in peanuts than in politics.

"If I become President," Jimmy told his audiences, "you may not always agree with what I do. I cannot promise that I'll always be right. I *can* promise that I will never be satisfied with less than the best.

"I will never tell a lie. I would never betray your trust in me."

Jimmy said that a government should be well organized and economical. Even more important, it should be honest and decent, not only with its own people, but with other countries.

With only six hours of sleep every night, Jimmy was often tired. When things didn't go right, it would be easy to become angry. Someone once asked him how he stayed calm.

"I just say a brief silent prayer," he answered. "I don't ask for myself, but just to let me understand what another's feelings might be."

The states began to have their primary elections to choose the candidate they would support at the national conventions. Early in 1976, Jimmy won the Democratic primary

Jimmy enjoys an ice cream cone while campaigning in Florida. He hopes for a win in the Florida primary.

in both Iowa and New Hampshire. In Massachusetts, however, Senator Henry Jackson of Washington won, while Jimmy came in fourth. He was tired and grumpy, but that night he and his staff stayed up until two o'clock in the morning. They were making plans to beat Jackson in Florida.

As the campaign progressed, Jimmy won some states and lost others. The Pennsylvania primary in April was a turning point. Jackson and the popular United States Senator from Minnesota, Hubert Humphrey, left the race.

Governor Jerry Brown of California entered the Maryland primary and won. By now Jimmy had won seventeen states, and was almost certain to become his party's presidential nominee.

The national Democratic Party convention was held in New York City in July, 1976. When Jimmy was introduced, there wasn't much applause. Many of the delegates were not happy. They wanted some of the other candidates to be nominated.

After a series of votes, Jerry Brown was still in the running. Two other possibilities were Morris Udall and Ellen McCormack. Jimmy won the final vote and became his party's choice. Even then, the applause was not very enthusiastic. He bagan to speak.

"My name is Jimmy Carter, and I'm running for President. . . . Our people are searching for new voices and new ideas and new leaders. . . . It is time for the people to run the government, and not the other way around. . . ."

By the time his speech was over, the delegates were cheering. Jimmy had won their confidence.

Senator Walter Mondale of Minnesota became his

Jimmy Carter and Walter Mondale, with their wives, Rosalynn and Joan, acknowledge the cheers of the crowd.

choice for vice-president. Both he and Jimmy started to campaign immediately. Everyone in the country had now heard of Jimmy Carter, but they were still asking questions. "What does he stand for?" "What will he do for us?"

Jimmy answered many of their questions on television as he debated with the Republican candidate, President Gerald Ford. He said that he planned to reorganize the government, and save the tax payers' money. He was going to try to see that everyone who wanted to work could find a job. He wanted to find new ways to save gas and oil.

Rosalynn did not always agree with everything he said. "I tell him what I think," she said. One of the things she didn't like was being called "Rosie" in public.

People noticed little things that Jimmy did. He carried his own suitcases, instead of waiting for someone else to do it.

Carter still carried his own luggage.

He stayed in private homes, instead of big hotels. During a magazine interview, he sewed up a rip in his coat.

He was often seen in jeans and T-shirts instead of business suits. When he was in Plains, he wore shorts and went barefoot. He found his own ways to relax—playing Frisbee with Amy, bouncing on a trampoline, playing baseball with Billy, having a fish fry, or walking through the fields with Rosalynn.

Thousands of people came to Plains. They bought "Jimmy-things," as Miss Lillian called the souvenirs in the stores. They drove into Billy's service station, and bought lemonade from Amy's stand. They visited Hugh Carter's antique store and his worm farm. They talked to Miss Lillian as she sat in her rocking chair.

"Jimmy's going to win or bust," she said.

The election was held on November 2. Jimmy spent the day in Plains. That night, before he left for Atlanta with Amy and Rosalynn, he thanked everyone who had helped him. Then he kissed Miss Lillian.

"Mama, I'm going to win," he said.

The results were close, but Jimmy did win by over a million and a half votes. Almost ninety percent of the Blacks in the country had voted for him.

The sun was rising as he flew back to Plains the next day. Four hundred people were waiting to greet him. Jimmy choked back tears of gratitude as he spoke to them.

"I think the sun's rising on a beautiful new day—a beautiful new spirit in America."

President-elect Jimmy Carter gets a hug from his mother during a victory celebration in Plains.

10

"Let Us Learn Together"

At noon on January 20, 1977, Jimmy repeated the oath of office. When he was finished, he was President Jimmy Carter, the thirty-ninth President of the United States. Over 150,000 people stood on the frosty grounds of the Capitol Building to hear his speech.

"This inauguration ceremony marks a new beginning, a new dedication within our government, and a new spirit among us all. A President may sense and proclaim that spirit, but only a people can provide it. . . . I pray that I can live up to your confidence and never disappoint you."

Jimmy and Rosalynn stepped into the waiting limousine, and the Inaugural Parade started. A few minutes later, the limousine stopped. The President and the First Lady got out, and began to walk up Pennsylvania Avenue

Jimmy Carter being sworn in as thirty-ninth President of the
United States.

President Jimmy Carter chose to walk the entire parade route following his inauguration. Here, he and Mrs. Carter, with their daughter Amy between them and other members of the family walking behind, pass along Pennsylvania Avenue.

toward the White House. Amy walked between them, with the rest of their family behind.

All along the one-and-a-half-mile walk, cries of delight rose from the crowd. "Will you look at that? He's walking!"

Jimmy was at his desk at 9:00 the following morning. Already, there were people waiting to see him, and many papers which needed to be read and signed. He barely had time to think about the big problems which needed to be solved. He had studied them for many weeks.

The President attends a foreign policy breakfast with Vice-President Mondale and Secretary of State Cyrus R. Vance.

One of the problems was the economic condition of the country. Jimmy planned to lower taxes, have government officials be more careful about how they spent the tax money, and help businessmen provide more jobs for people.

Another problem was the high cost of health care. He felt that people should not have to suffer poor health just because they cannot afford to go to a doctor or a hospital. He wanted to provide some form of national health insurance.

Jimmy also had to find ways to help the nation's big cities. Many of the people who lived in places such as New York, Chicago, and Los Angeles needed jobs, better houses, and protection from crime.

To solve another problem, Jimmy would have to talk to the leaders of the Soviet Union. He wanted an agreement about cutting down the number of nuclear weapons. He also

wanted the Russian leaders to give their people more freedom and justice. Jimmy believes that no matter where people live, they should be treated fairly. "Human rights are the property of all people," he said.

A major problem was that of finding new ways to provide fuel and energy for the nation's businesses, homes, schools, and transportation. Jimmy planned an energy bill. In it he wanted to encourage Americans to stop wasting gas, to develop solar and nuclear power, and to use coal instead of oil. But the main purpose of the bill was to free the nation from having to depend on oil from foreign countries.

He had been president for only a week when the energy problem became more crucial than ever. The eastern part of the United States was overcome by the coldest winter in many years. Jimmy asked people not to keep their houses so warm, and suggested that businesses close down an extra day a week. Everyone had to save fuel, or there would not be enough to go around.

"With the exception of preventing war, this is the greatest challenge our nation will face during our lifetime," he said of the energy shortage.

Jimmy wrote his energy bill, and presented it to Congress. If Congress approved this bill, many of his ideas would become laws.

Almost everyone agreed that the energy problem must be solved, but no one agreed on how to solve it. A Department of Energy was created, but Congress refused to approve many of Jimmy's other plans. The new President found that he had to give up some things which he wanted, in

The President holds a coal strike meeting with his senior White House staff.

order to get just a part of his plan accepted.

When he had been in office for only a few months, the country's coal miners went on strike. Congress had given the President the power to order the miners to return to work. Their leaders and the men who owned the coal mines could then talk about their disagreements while the miners were doing their job. However, the miners refused to obey the President's order. Thus, the United States went into another winter with no energy bill, plus a shortage of coal. Spring arrived before the mines were in operation again.

Jimmy had more success with his Panama Canal Zone treaties. The Panama Canal Zone is a strip of land on both sides of the canal. This land and the canal itself are owned by the United States. In 1903, the United States had signed a treaty with Panama in which our country would have control of the Panama Canal and the Canal Zone forever. Jimmy thought this treaty was unfair. He believed that Panama should own the canal and zone. Some people agreed with him, but were afraid to give up either the zone or the canal. They felt the Panama Canal is very important to our national security, since it enables ships to get from one coast to the other quickly.

In March, 1978, the first of the new treaties was approved by the United States Senate. The people of Panama were closer to gaining control of the canal and the Canal Zone.

Jimmy was also working on other problems. He wanted to reform the election laws, so people could vote more easily. He was concerned about finding ways to give welfare money only to the people who really needed it. He wanted businessmen to be more honest with their customers. However, his request for a Consumer Protection Agency was turned down by Congress.

The illegal alien problem also needed a solution. There were many foreign people in the United States, who did not have permission to be here. Thousands of them were Mexicans, who crossed our Southern border every year because there were not enough jobs for them in Mexico. Jimmy wanted to help the ones who were already in the United States, while preventing more from coming in.

In the Cabinet Room of the White House, Israeli Prime Minister Menachem Begin (left) and his aides, face President Carter (right) and other officials. Two days of talks were being held in an attempt to ease the tense situation in the Middle East.

One of Jimmy's greatest worries is the threat of war in the Middle East. The state of Israel, homeland of many Jewish people, had fought three wars with the nearby Arab countries during the past 30 years. Yet another war threatens to break out between these countries and Israel. Jimmy met with the leaders of many countries, especially Menachem Begin of Israel and Anwar Sadat of Egypt, one of the Arab countries. They hope to find a peaceful solution to the problem.

Meanwhile members of Jimmy's family were helping him in their own ways. They traveled to places where the President had not time to go. Chip made a trip to China to meet with leaders there. Rosalynn traveled to many different parts of the United States. She wanted to find out what people thought about the President, and to see what they wanted him to do.

"I want people to feel that the government is theirs," she said.

The Jimmy Carter family find time to pose for a portrait. Left to right—Jack and Judy with their son, Jason; Jeff and Annette; the President and Mrs. Carter and Amy; Chip and Caron with their son, James Earl IV.

She visited the slum areas of Washington, D.C. and determined to take some action.

"It all seems so hopeless," she said. "But I really believe that something can be done in the cities if we can get people interested in working together."

Rosalynn also went to South America to carry the President's message of concern and friendship to the people there.

Many presidents have not taken the time to explain to the people just what their plans were. They have not asked the people what they want. To do this, Jimmy has continued

Each January, the President presents his State of the Union message to Congress.

President Carter holds a press conference.

Left to right: Speaker of the House Thomas P. O'Neill, Jr. of Massachusetts, President Carter, Senate Majority Leader Robert Byrd of West Virginia.

his practice of having radio call-in shows. He attends town meetings, and stays overnight in people's homes. He talks to newspaper reporters twice a month, and appears on television often.

As Jimmy's first year in office ended, some people liked the changes he was trying to make. However, others thought that he was doing too much too fast. They said he tried to do too much by himself, and that he made mistakes because he didn't understand national politics.

Jimmy himself found that he had to start working more closely with the members of Congress. He had to understand their special concerns. He realized that even if his ideas were good, it takes time to make big changes when they affect millions of people.

During his first year as President, Jimmy made two trips to Europe. He also traveled to various cities in the United States. Most of his working days are spent in the Oval Office. He is at his desk by 7:00 in the morning and calls the first ninety minutes his "quiet time." Whoever disturbs him during this time must be prepared to pay. *"Really* pay," says, Jody Powell, his press secretary.

At 8:30, the first of many people visit his office. All day long, he talks to people such as Vice-President Mondale, cabinet members, foreign officials, congressmen, businessmen, and labor leaders. Jimmy does not allow even one minute to be spent on unnecessary details.

"Every day gone is a day wasted if you haven't crammed in every single bit of accomplishment you can," he once said.

In addition to appointments and meetings, Jimmy must find time to read three hundred letters and documents every day. He orders his staff to use simple words, and not too many of them. As he reads, he scribbles in the margins. "Go ahead." "I agree." "NO!"

He circles mistakes in grammar, spelling, and arithmetic. At first people had trouble spelling Zbigniew Brzezinski, the name of the national security advisor. Jimmy ordered everyone to learn the correct spelling immediately.

In his private study at the White House, the President works on a speech which will be televised nationally.

The President holds a regular Monday morning cabinet meeting.

At 7:00 in the evening, Jimmy eats dinner with Amy and Rosalynn, then returns to his office. Until eleven or twelve o'clock, he reads more papers, talks to advisors, or studies.

The President's job is hard, and his days are long. Jimmy manages to stay calm most of the time. There are occasions, however, when his blue eyes turn dark and icy, and his face reddens. When that happens, his staff knows they should leave him alone. "That stare" means that Jimmy is "whizzed off" about something.

Jimmy can be seen plodding barefoot through the halls of the White House. He attends most of his meetings wearing old jeans, polo shirts and sweaters. He is most comfortable in those clothes, and he sees no reason to be uncomfortable, even if he is President.

★ ★ ★ ★ ★ ★ ★ ★

Some day, historians will write about Jimmy Carter. At that time, they well be able to judge how good a President he was. For now, it is enough to know that most Americans believe that he is an honest man. He is trying to give Americans what they want and need. And he is learning from his mistakes.

Jimmy Carter knows he is only one man, and that he needs the help of the people to do his job. He asked for that help in his Inaugural Address. "Your strength can compensate for my weakness, and your wisdom can help minimize my mistakes. Let us learn together and laugh together and work together and pray together, confident that in the end we will triumph together in the right."

Index